# I

# AM

# A

# SURVIVOR

# TOO

### BY

### PATRICIA ANN BROWNE

Argus Enterprises International, Inc
New Jersey***North Carolina

*I am a Survivor Too*© 2011  All
rights reserved by Argus Enterprises
International, Inc.

A-Argus Better Book Publishers, LLC

For information:
A-Argus Better Book Publishers, LLC
9001 Ridge Hill Street
Kernersville, North Carolina 27285
www.a-argusbooks.com

ISBN: 978-0-9846348-9-7

Book Cover designed by Dubya

Printed in the United States of America

# Forward

I am not a professional writer and have never even thought about writing a book of any kind. That would have been the very last thing I would have ever considered. You will immediately know that I am not a professional by the way this book is written.

I didn't even finish high school; at least, I didn't as a teen. I did go back and get my diploma after I became an adult, but that's a different story. Nevertheless, I do love to read and I read a lot of different kinds of books; murder, mystery, horror, western, science fiction. You name it. I am not however, very much into Self-Help books. Don't believe in them very much and I have my doubts if most of them are accurate. At least, I once didn't think they were real.

Then, one day while browsing the Barnes and Noble website, I ran across a book entitled "My Sister and I: We Are Survivors" by J. Jackson Owensby. At first, I was shocked. Then, I was mesmerized by the subject of childhood sexual abuse. That subject just hit too close to home, so I started to scroll away from the site when something stopped me. What had really captured my attention was a customer review from a character with the title "PinkFreud", who felt that it was inappropriate for the author to use the precise words of the women whose tale that he was relating and evidently "PinkFreud" felt it was wrong of the two women to relate their story to a future in-law. That made me stop and read the complete review. And then I read other consumer reviews, mostly good, a few bad. And I started to boil.

Who is that person to judge anyone? Has he/she ever been the victim of sexual abuse? Was he/she molested as a child by an insidious adult that continued to attack the victim? Has he/she ever sat and listened to people pour their very hearts out; listened to their cries of anguish? He/she felt that the story should be edited to make the book easier for the reader to read. Easier? Easier, my foot! Have any of the critics who pooh-poohed the author and the women ever sat and talked to a victim of sexual abuse, ever listened to a victim of sexual abuse? Especially a victim of continual sexual abuse from their childhood onward? A victim of their own family? I didn't think so.

Well, try it, smart guy, or smart gal. When you have walked in the shoes of those two magnificent women and sat in the chair of the future father-in-law and heard that horrifying story about how deranged adults (yes, adults, meaning more than one) can degrade and abase a child—yes, an infant, then make your comments. When you understand that infant translate as baby, toddler, preschooler, then you will understand that at the age of four, a child is still an infant. When you experience for yourself the degradation of being a helpless sexual victim in the hands of a malicious monster, then you can judge, then you can spout off, then you can say something meaningful. Until then, f.o., if you know what I mean. (Sorry, Ms. editor)

But I should say thank you. Thank you, "PinkFreud. Thank you very much.

Thank you and the other critics who felt that the language should be cleaned up so that it wouldn't grate so harshly on the reader's consciousness, make it easier for you to read. Yeah. Thank you because your comments galvanized me into action. Made me determined to tell my side of the story. Your comments, your snide, spiteful remarks made this book possible. No, not just possible. Necessary.

Without your sarcastic, non-feeling comments, I would l never have had the nerve to even start this manuscript, much less try to have it published.

I will likewise say thank you to those who understood. Understood not only the author's efforts, but understood the purpose of the book, the real reason why those two valiant women braved the derisive world and chose someone who would believe them. Wise choice, girls. Your stories are just too horrific, too damning, too unreal to be real. Are men really that much of animal. Surely you exaggerate. Not everyone would believe.

I do. As they say, been there, done that. Got the t-shirt and the hat. And the rest of it too.

And yes, I did buy the book. But I ordered the printed version. I wanted something solid to hold on to. Had to wait a while, but it was well worth it.

As I said, I'm not a professional writer so I'm leaving it up to the editor to put this book in order. No, I don't want my language cleaned up. This is me. and too bad if you don't like me. And yes, I am using my real name.

And thank you, Deena and you, Starla. Your courage put me to shame. You made me realize that I am not alone, that what happened to me wasn't my thought, that I am a person – a whole person – and that nothing anyone did to me makes me less of a person. So, with kudos to you ladies, I start my story.

Patricia Ann Browne

# Part One

I am a survivor of childhood sexual abuse.

How would you like to be placed in a day-care facility almost as soon as you are born? Take it from me; it isn't pleasant being a baby without a mother's tender loving care.

I'm not sure how much it had to do with the evil things happened to me, but I came from a single parent family. My father was killed in an automobile accident just before I was born. Evidence showed that he was driving under the influence, which it appears he often did, and he ran headlong into a Greyhound bus between Charlotte, NC and Chester, SC. To compound the loss, the insurance agency (you're in good hands), refused to pay for his death, as the alcohol he had in his system was the major cause of the accident. My mother didn't have the money or the knowledge to fight, so we were left destitute.

My mother had to go to work to support me and my two older brothers. Dave was fourteen years old when I was born and my second brother, Carl, was twelve. My parents didn't plan on having any more children so I guess that you could say that I was just another accident caused by my father's drinking. Turns out that he had raped my mother after coming home one night drunk once again…that is, if a husband can be guilty of raping his wife. At any rate, that was

the last time they had sex as my father
was killed a couple of weeks afterwards.
Unfortunately, his seed had proved quite
strong and my mother proved most
fertile, so along I came some eight
months later. At this time of my life, I am
surprised that my mother didn't abort me,
but I think it may be because she just
didn't have the money. It certainly wasn't
because of her belief, nor because she
really wanted another kid to feed.

It was about the time that I was
two years old that my mother began to
consider leaving me home with my
brothers. She felt that they were old
enough (Dave at sixteen and Carl at
fourteen) to babysit me and take care of
themselves. I believe the only thing that
stopped her was that Dave was one of the
more popular students in high school and

was a sports star in basketball, baseball and basketball. Mother must have been hoping that Dave would get a scholarship for college, or perhaps start playing professional sports. He was always saying that he was going to make it big and when he did he would be taking care of all of us. But that kind of luck or success wasn't destined for my family. During the last game of the season, Carl was a sophomore and the star running back on his high school team. He was tackled by one of the other team's defensive players and his right knee was destroyed. In fact, the damage was so bad that the doctors had to do a total knee replacement. Luckily the school's insurance paid for everything and in addition sent Dave a monthly check for the disability. At least, I think the money came from the insurance company.

Anyway, Dave was never the same afterwards, limping as he walked and unable to run.

Dave was never the same after that. Although I was barely two, I knew something had gone wrong with my older brother. No longer was he the cheerful, playing, teasing brother that I had come to love. He just didn't seem the same, morose, sad and always gruff. He didn't play with me in the same way, tossing me into the air and ticking me, blowing his breath under my chin and across my neck. In fact, as I remember, he rarely picked me up and never held me. I could only sense that he was different, hurt in some way. But I didn't understand.

Dave never finished high school. At some time he must have dropped out.

Apparently many of his friends were fair-weather friends and now that he wasn't a star, his friends moved along to someone else. And, as time went by, Dave became more of a stranger to me, completely different, always grouchy and touchy, even mean to me and to Carl at times.

Dave didn't have a job to go to, so he was around the house most of the time. My mother took advantage to his presence and decided to use him as a baby sitter. I don't believe that our mother ever tried to get Dave to go back to school. In fact, I now believe that she was happy that he wasn't going to school. Dave could take care of me and Carl while she slept and she wouldn't have to pay a day-care for me.

Although I didn't really understand at first, I thought it was great. I
wasn't going into a place where there
were just a bunch of strangers. I was able
to stay home with my brother, who I was
sure loved me and would soon get over
his grouchy mood and be the playmate
that he had always been.

Our mother worked on the third
shift at the local textile mill, one of the
few that hadn't closed down and moved
to Mexico or China. At least, not at that
time. Mother would start to work at ten
o'clock at night and get off at six o'clock
the next morning. She would get home
somewhere around seven and go
immediately to bed, often without saying
a word to me or my brothers, even we
were mostly awake. She was so tired she
would just collapse and we were not

allowed to open the door to her room lest we awaken her. That was an iron-clad rule that I had learned early, not to disturb her sleep. Even as a small infant, if she woke up, someone would get a spanking. And that was usually me. Sometimes she would take a belt and whip Carl, but I don't ever remember her striking Dave at all, not with anything. It was just Carl and me. When I was a little older, around three or four, she would use the belt on me, often leaving welts on my legs and back. A few times with that and you learn not to make noise that would wake her.

Carl had become one of the most popular students in his high school. It turned out that he was even more popular than Dave had been and he was also a much better athlete than Dave. Carl didn't seem to rub it in but it grated on Dave, much more than anyone knew and more than I could understand at my age. I didn't know what jealousy was but I was beginning to learn.

It got almost to the point that anything Carl did would make Dave even more morose and angry. Little by little, it seemed that Dave was becoming more remote from us. I didn't know what was happening, but I knew it was something bad. It even got to the point that Dave and Carl were not even speaking to one another. But our mother didn't seem to notice, as she was almost never around.

Mother would sleep until five or six o'clock in the afternoon. Then she would get up, make her bed, and begin to prepare supper for all of us. That was the only meal that we spent together, although more and more often Carl was away from home at a ball game. I now realize that he deliberately stayed away, not wanting to get into yet another argument with Dave, and not wanting to hear our mother tell us what a good man Dave was to be taking care of us when she wasn't there. Still, even this didn't make Dave any happier, and in fact seemed as if it were rubbing salt in his wounds. It was hard for Dave to find a job as the problems with his knee continued. He wasn't able to stand for any spell of time, nor could he walk very far without having to sit down. The fact that he had not finished high school didn't help him at all, although he did try working at McDonalds, but his leg wouldn't let him do what he needed to do, so he was terminated.

I don't remember much about that time of my life, after all, a three-year-old child doesn't know very much. I do know that my fourth birthday was coming up soon, and I was looking forward to it. I knew that my mother would bake a cake; I could remember the candles on the small cake she had made for my third birthday. Even at that age, I was aware that there would be no birthday gifts, as we had no money to spend on toys or such, so I wasn't disappointed. Still, the cake was a banana nut cake, which was my favorite. And I was allowed to have two slices since it as my birthday. I even was allowed to blow out the candles all by myself. Since there was only four, it didn't take much, but I did have to blow two times so it wasn't a surprise that I didn't get my wish. Still, I wasn't too disappointed, it seems as if my mother and Dave and Carl were much nicer. At least, there were no arguments on that day.

That was the last year of my childhood as things were about to change.

Dave had tried to work in construction, but his knee made it so painful that he couldn't work. Our mother insisted he stay home, telling him that if he did get a job, he would likely lose his monthly disability check and the free medical care he was getting from the Social Services. I didn't know what social services were but came to realize it was welfare. Our mother said that if Dave lost his check and the social services, she would not be able to support us and could not pay for the medical attention that Dave was getting. In actuality, the medical attention was mostly in the form of drugs, pain-killers that Dave took almost like aspirins.

It was about that time that Dave began drinking. Beer, mostly, but on occasion he would drink wine or something else. At first, it didn't seem to make a lot of difference, Dave would just get tired in the afternoon and lay on the sofa and sleep while I would watch television. The only programs I liked were cartoons and some shows with animals, although there was one with a man named after an animal. I think I remember his name as Captain Kangaroo or something like that. He was a funny old man.

Dave began waking up from his afternoon nap – or at least that is what he called it – and started watching the programs with me. I thought he was getting better as he would laugh at some of the cartoons, especially Mickey Mouse and Popeye. I was happy, because sitting on the floor was hard. With Dave awake and sitting up watching the television, I could sit on the sofa and snuggle up against him. Mother always kept the heat turned low, and in the wintertime it would get cold. Snuggling up to Dave with a blanket made me feel warm and safe, especially when Dave would put his arm around me and hug me. He would also rub my back and shoulders and sometimes my legs. This helped keep me warm and made me feel good. It seemed that Dave was coming out of his "black funk" as Carl called it. I was happy. But things were about to change, and not for the better.

~*~

During the next few months after my fourth birthday, Dave began to watch more and more television with me. If I didn't climb up on the sofa, he would pick me up and place me beside him, covering me with my favorite blanket. I didn't really care for the television programs he was watching, some game shows and some soap operas, something called "General Hospital" or "As The World Turns." But I was happy that Dave wanted me to sit beside him. I had missed him when he was sad.

Now he would have a beer or a drink in the morning but didn't try to sleep in the afternoon. He spent most of the time watching the television, but he would have a beer can or a glass of wine or something else while he was watching the television, while holding his arm around me and hugging me. When he didn't have a glass in his hand, he would use both hands to rub me, massaging my shoulders and back. He would also rub my legs, starting at my feet and going up to above my knees. I didn't say anything as his hands were warm and his rubbing was soft and gentle. He didn't pinch or squeeze or anything. Many times after rubbing me, Dave would get off the sofa and go into the bathroom in the hall. He would stay in there for a long time and I would hear a few noises. Then he would come back out and sit down on the sofa beside me. Most of the time after coming back from the bathroom, he would just lean against me and go to sleep. I would sit there, not moving, not wanting to wake Dave up. Anyway, he wasn't that heavy as he was only leaning a little.

This went on for some time and then Dave began to talk to me as he would rub my back or legs. He would say "Does this feel good?" "Am I hurting you?" "Do you want me to do this?" Of course it did feel good and no, he wasn't hurting me. And it was okay if it made him feel good, although sometimes the rubbing would cause my skin to burn. Even so, I wouldn't ask him to stop because I didn't want to hurt his feelings.

Things changed a little. In addition to talking to me and asking questions, Dave began to kiss the top of my head as he would rub me. That seemed a little strange. Still, I wanted my big brother to feel good and to like me, so I didn't say anything. Dave would rub me, and kiss the top of my head, sometimes kissing it for a long time. Then he would jump up, push me away and hurry into the bathroom. I didn't know what to make of that, I guess I just thought the beer and other stuff made him have to go in a hurry.

One day, while rubbing my legs, Dave began to kiss my forehead and the corner of my eyes. His hands rubbing me became a little strong, so I said, "Dave, take it easy. You're doing it too hard. It's hurting." I tried to move away, but Dave's arms were wrapped around me.

"I'll take it easy," he said and his hands slowed down and became a lot softer. That didn't hurt so much, so I settled back down.

After that, Dave would just sit on the sofa and have me sit beside him, still with the blanket. (My birthday was November, so the weather was rather cold). We would just sit there, with no television, me snuggled up against him and his arms around me, his hands rubbing me. Mostly, he rubbed my back and shoulders, and sometimes my legs, but now it seemed that he was rubbing my legs much more often and for much longer. His hands were now rubbing above my knees on my thighs and sometimes it seemed that his fingers would brush against my other parts. He would quickly move his hands lower on my legs but his hands continued to climb until they were on my thighs again. At that point, Dave would take my thighs in his large hands and massage them rather than rubbing. All the time he would be asking me if I liked it, if it was making me feel good, if it was okay with me. And of course it wasn't hurting me and making him like me so I kept quiet. Almost every day, Dave was having to make a trip to the bathroom, and almost every time when he came back, he would take a nap, as if something in the bathroom was making him tired and sleepy.

Gradually, Dave's rubbing began to spread all over my body. He would rub across my chest with the palm of his hands, probing my belly-button and pinching my nipples. He would ask if that felt good, and I would say it didn't really hurt. The truth is that it did hurt and I didn't want him to continue, but I was afraid that he would not like me anymore and that he would become the way he was before, so I didn't say much. And he continued.

Now it seems clear that what Dave was doing was taking a little more liberty from day to day, not wanting to scare a four-year-old. But he couldn't seem to keep his hands off me. We would spend almost all day every day, sitting on the sofa, me with a blanket around me and Dave's hands under the blanket, massaging, rubbing, pinching, probing.

As Dave was home all day, it seemed only natural that he would do the household chores, washing clothes, cleaning. He would iron any clothes, especially the ones that Carl wore to school. And he would wash my clothes as well. Then, in the mornings, he would help me dress, choosing what I should wear. On many days, because I would be under a blanket on the sofa, I would only have a thin chemise and my panties to wear. And sometimes, if the chemise wasn't clean, I would actually not have on a shirt at all. I didn't really notice, but I now realize that after Dave began rubbing over most of my body that my chemise was often dirty and most of the time I would sit under the blanket with only my panties on.

One day I didn't have my chemise. Dave had started rubbing me just a little while after breakfast. This time his hands traveled up my legs from my ankles to the junction of my legs. I could feel his hands on my genitals. That shocked me because it seemed to be wrong.

"Don't do that." I said and took his hands to move them away.

"Don't do what?" Dave's voice sounded strange.

"Don't touch my pee-pee." Well, what else would a four-year-old call it?

Dave growled something and jumped up. Not saying a word, he turned and stomped out of the house and didn't come back for several hours.

I immediately felt sorry and scared, afraid that something that I had done had chased him away. If so, my mother would beat me good. After the

33

first few minutes, I was afraid that Dave
had left for good, so I began crying. I
guess I cried myself to sleep because the
next sound I heard was the door
slamming as Dave returned. I was afraid
that he would say something to our
mother and that she would whip me. She
always told me to behave and to mind
Dave and if Dave told me to do
something that I had better do it or suffer
the consequences. I knew what the
consequences would be, -another
whipping with the belt or a stick. That
had happened too often and I didn't want
another beating which I was sure to get if
Dave told her I was being mean. She
always believed anything Dave told her.

Dave didn't say anything though,
but he didn't sit on the sofa with me
either, although I had hardly moved since

he left. The rest of the day he seemed a little surly, only growling if someone spoke to him. When our mother spoke to him, he was much more like his old self, only short with Carl and me. Mostly me. *What did I do wrong?*

The next day it seemed like everything was back to normal. My chemise was clean and dry, so I put it on, grabbed my blanket and sat on the sofa. I was holding my breath, afraid that Dave would still be mad, but he took his place beside me, put his arm around me and seemed to forget that I had made him mad. His rubbing, or I guess his stroking, started, but he stayed away from my genitals, although I was not going to say a word even if he touched me there. He didn't and I was glad.

Patricia Ann Browne

For the rest of the week, we continued in that fashion, me sitting meekly, willing to accept whatever Dave wanted, while he remained much the same. But then once again his hands seemed to reach higher on my legs and thighs and the ends of his fingers would brush against my panties. I didn't say a word, afraid that he would get mad again.

It wasn't but a few days more until Dave was once again placing his hand firmly on my genitals, cupping and holding while his other hand would stroke my hair, my neck or my chest. He would kiss my forehead, my neck, my ears. And when I didn't have a chemise, he would kiss all over my shoulders, my chest and my belly. All the time, Dave would be murmuring words, mostly words that I couldn't understand. But some, like "That's okay", "Take it easy", "Please let me", "Be good to me and I'll be good to you" were words that I could understand but that made no sense to me. Dave's hugs grew stronger as he would press me tight against him while his hand was rubbing my genitals. Actually that made me want to pee, but I was afraid to say anything, so I just sat there. After a while, Dave would get up again and go to the bathroom.

I noticed that more and more often, my chemise would be in the dirty clothes and I wouldn't have a top to wear, so I would have to sit under the blanket with no shirt. Dave's stroking became more firm and he was touching me all over. One day, I felt Dave's fingers crawling under the edge of my panties leg. He began rubbing me harder and when I tried to twist away, he pulled me tight against him. I was frightened as it seemed that something came over Dave.

"Don't move," he said. "This will feel good." With that, Dave put his lips on my lips and began to kiss me hard. I could hardly breathe and tried to open my mouth to ask him to stop. He pushed his tongue into my mouth and at the same time tore my panties off. He pushed me down on the sofa and crawled between my legs. I couldn't move, I couldn't resist. I didn't know what was happening and couldn't even cry out. I felt a sudden sharp pain stab me that felt like a hot knife stabbing me. I tried to scream but couldn't. Everything went black.

# Part 2

I guess that I must have fainted from the pain. When I woke up, I was by myself. I was lying on top of my blanket on the sofa and I was not wearing any clothes. I tried to move and it really hurt. Looking down at my belly, I could see blood on my belly and legs. *What had happened? Why was I bleeding?* I tried to stand up and it really hurt. It felt as if I had been split in two. I knew something was wrong, but had no idea what. I did know that I needed to clean up the sofa and me, and to put some clothes on because it was almost time for our mother to get out of bed. I don't know what she would do if she saw the mess, but I knew she would blame me. And that meant another beating. I went into the bathroom and scrubbed the blood off my legs and belly. *God, there was a lot of it.* There was some other junk on my legs but I didn't know what it was. Know what it turned out to be, but I didn't learn that until later. Then I found another pair of panties and a shirt and put them on. Going back to clean the sofa, I found my torn panties lying on the floor, ripped apart. That made me angry. Those were favorite panties, with little strawberry shortcake designs on them, and now they were ruined. I made up my mind that I was going to tell our mother just as soon as she got out of bed.

However, before that happened, Dave came back into the house from somewhere. I guess he had been to the store as he was carrying a bag full of beer. He didn't say a word to me, just a strange smile. I was so mad at him for ripping my favorite underwear that I wouldn't talk to him, either. I just waited for our mother to get out of bed.

When our mother finally came out of her bedroom, I ran to her and spoke up immediately. "Mommy, Dave hurt me."

She said, "If Dave hurt you, he must have had a good reason. Just be good and he won't have to hurt you."

"But, Mom! Dave tore up my favorite panties, he hurt…."

"Just shut up, Patty. If Dave hurt you, you must have deserved it. Anyway, take care of your own clothes and Dave won't tear them."

*Take care of my own clothes at the age of four?*

"But Mom! Dave stuck his thing in…"

"Patricia Ann, I said for you to shut up. I don't want to hear any more out of you."

"But…." I stopped talking when she slapped me across the mouth. She slapped really hard.

"I told you. Dave is taking care of you. You just behave yourself and do what Dave tells you to do, and everything will be okay. If you want a beating, you just keep on."

That pretty much ended the conversation. She just didn't want to listen, she didn't want to know what was happening. She closed both ears. (It wasn't until much later in life that I learned from relatives that my mother had been the unwilling victim of incest with *her* brother, and that Dave was the result of that incest, with my mother having to marry my father when she found out she was pregnant with her brother's baby. She hadn't wanted to get married, but at the time you just didn't have a baby unless you were married. At least not in our "neck of the woods" as they say. I don't think my mother had any good times with my father, he was much older and not really much of a catch. But, being pregnant, she didn't really have much of a choice, and just grabbed the first person who smiled at her).

Dave just looked at me with a smirky look on his face. I was old enough to know that meant trouble.

And I was right. The next morning as I woke up, I was yanked from my warm bed by Dave. When I tried to protest he told me to "get your ass on the sofa right now. If you don't I'll tell Mom that you are being bad. Then she will beat you and I will still get you."

Scared and shaking, I had no choice but to go to the sofa. Before I got there, Dave shouted, "And take off those clothes, I want you naked." Sobbing, I obeyed. I removed all my clothes and climbed up on the sofa. But now my blanket was missing, in fact there was nothing on the sofa except for a couple of pillows.

Then Dave came out of the bathroom, walking toward the sofa. He didn't have on any clothes. As he sat down on the sofa, he grabbed me.

And then it started. Again and again.

Over the next two years, it was almost every day. Dave would wake me up and then make me go to the sofa. Sometimes he would let me watch television while he did things to me and at other times he would refuse.

After several weeks went by, Dave wanted to try something new. He wanted me to kiss his thing. There was no way I was going to do that. He told me that the only reason woman was on the earth was to satisfy the man, that the woman was not good for anything else. He said that any woman who could not satisfy a man was no good and that all girl children were no good until they learned how to please a man.

When my mother got out of bed that afternoon, I tried again to tell her what Dave was doing to me, but again she would not listen to a word. When I started crying, she reached for a switch and began beating me with it while Dave just stood and watched, with a big smile on his face.

It wasn't long before Dave had me doing anything he wanted. There wasn't any way I could refuse. If I tried, he would tell my mother and then she would beat me and I would have to do it anyway. After a while, I just gave up. Whatever Dave wanted, Dave got.

I was looking forward to the time when I would be six years old. I knew that I would be allowed to go to school and that would get me away from the house. And, I thought, away from Dave.

It didn't work out that way. When it was time for me to enroll in school, it was Dave, not my mother that took me to the school office. And it was Dave who told me that if I told anyone at school what he was doing that he would beat me, and that our mother would beat me and that no one would believe me. He also told me that what he was doing was done in most families, but those families kept it quiet because they didn't want anyone else to know.

Going to school did get me away from Dave for most of the day, but when I got home from school, he made up for it. Every day. Sometimes he even crawled in my bed and had at me after our mother left for work at 9:30 at night.

All the while that Dave was after me, he kept telling me that it would feel good, that I would get to where I liked it. He told me that good women enjoyed sex as much as a man and that sooner or later I would start having fun. That was a lie. Dave continued to assault me until I was sixteen, twelve years of almost continuous sexual assault by Dave and by others, and there was not one single moment that I actually enjoyed it. Even after the pain stopped, there was no pleasure at all, no good feeling. Not even when I was married, but that happened later.

At school, I felt that all of the other students were looking at me as if I was something weird, something or someone different. I couldn't see any difference when I looked in a mirror, but that didn't reassure me. I was certain that the other students knew that something was wrong with me, that I was being used and manipulated by my brother. I shunned contact with the other children, remaining in the classroom and studying during play periods so that I wouldn't have to face the other children. If I must say so myself, I was a quick learner and an excellent student, at least at first. My grades were at the top of the class and I felt that I had finally done something on my own. But then Dave bought a car.

We lived close to a mile from the school where I had to attend. For the first six grades, transportation was furnished by a bus. I didn't really mind the bus because the other students were busy with each other and no one paid any attention to me. I could get lost in the group. But after Dave bought the car, he decided that he would drive me to school every morning and pick me up in the afternoon. And that meant he wanted me to play with him and have oral sex with him on the way to school and on the way home.

Now, I know the other children thought I was strange. Sometimes I would come into the classroom with spots on my dress or in my hair caused by Dave. I tried to make sure that I went to the bathroom before entering the classroom, but there were times when that Dave made me so late there wasn't time to get refreshed.

Now, years later, I wonder what the teachers thought? If they noticed they didn't say anything. Neither did the other children, but I still believe that some of them knew something, if not everything that was happening to me.

Needless to say, with Dave's constant attention, my grades hit the skids, going from the top to the bottom in a short while. My teacher asked what was my problem, why was I not doing well, why was I not turning in my homework as I had been doing before, and I just didn't have an answer.

I wasn't doing well because I didn't want to do well. If I was going to spend my lifetime having to satisfy some man, I didn't need good grades, in fact, I didn't need school at all. But with my mother working, the school wouldn't allow home schooling, although Dave tried his best to get them to approve him as a home teacher. I'm certain that one of the reasons they refused was that Dave had not completed high school. If he had done so, there is no telling what the school authorities would have done and there is no way to tell what would have happened.

So Dave just continued to drive me to school and pick me up every day.

Many days I tried to be sick, but soon found out that I would have less trouble by going to school than I would if I stayed home. Being sick didn't keep Dave off me, and at least during school hours, I was safe.

Would you believe that a lot of my classmates were jealous of me? Jealous because I had a brother who would bring me to school every day and then pick me up in the afternoon. Jealous that I didn't have to wait for the bus, or have to push and shove just to have a seat. I could hear them whisper their little snide remarks about "a prima donna" with her own private car and driver. If they only knew. I would have gladly exchanged places with any one of them. But they didn't know, and I couldn't tell.

It wasn't long after Dave bought his car that he began to smoke. I didn't know what he was smoking but it smelled awful, a sweet-sour stench. And his breath. Between the beer and wine and other stuff and the smoking, his breath stunk. When he would try to kiss me, I would literally gag and almost vomit. That only earned me a clout upside my head, so I learned to hold my breath. Fortunately his kissing was now short and hard. I don't think he would have appreciated it if I vomited into his mouth. Would have made us even maybe for the stuff he put into my mouth.

Anyway, every afternoon, Dave would smoke some strange kind of cigarettes. They were short and stubby and I saw Dave actually roll one of them. He had some paper and what looked like tobacco and he would roll the tobacco up in the paper, lick one edge to make it stick together and then twist the ends together. Then he would light the thing and just lay back and smoke. The good part about it is that while he was smoking that cigarette, he wasn't bothering me.

At the age of six, I had learned a lot from listening Dave on the telephone and from hearing kids in my school talk. Especially the black kids. They seemed to know a lot more and would talk about such things as "pot", "hash" and other strange names. It was only when I got a little older that I understood what they actually meant. And it was only after I started thinking about writing my story that I could sit down and remember a lot of the things that happened at that time. Still, there was a lot that I have forgotten

and a lot more that I don't really want to
remember, but after I talked to the editor
at the publishing house that did My Sister
and I: We Are Survivors, I did promise to
do the best I could to tell the full and
complete story, the good with the bad.
Unfortunately, it was mostly bad.

Over a period of time, Dave kept
smoking. Smoking in the morning, which
I thought was good because he left me
alone on the way to school. There were a
lot of mornings when he couldn't – or
wouldn't – get up and I would have to
ride the bus. I was happy when that
happened, even though almost none of
the kids would talk to me on the bus.
Still, I could hear their sarcastic barbs
about the prima donna who had to ride
the bus. They all though it would bring
me down to earth and I would realize that

I wasn't as good as I seemed to think I was. It hurt. But it was good to be away from Dave, even if it were just a little while. Still, almost every day after school, Dave would be sitting in his car and start blowing his horn as the kids walked out of the school building.

Dave would smoke in the afternoon and sometimes he would take a short nap. But most of the time, he would just lie there, looking at me, and then he would make a gesture. I quickly learned what he wanted by each gesture, because if I didn't do something or if I did something wrong, that would earn another clout upside my head, and I don't mean a little love tap, either. It hurt. But then, as I said, I was a pretty fast learner even before I was seven years old.

Dave would take a puff of his cigarette and blow the smoke into my face and up my nose. It stunk. "You'll like it." He kept saying that I would like it. Never happened. The only thing that smoke did was to make me cough and want to throw up.

Sometime after Dave began smoking, there would be people coming to our house. We lived in a double-wide trailer home back in some woods a little off the main road. Most of the time we never saw anyone at all. It was only after Dave began smoking that these people would come by. Some of them were older men or older women. Some were teenagers, coming alone or in groups. It was always the same. They wouldn't stay long, only a few minutes. Dave would go outside and talk to them, which was okay with me because I would be left by myself in the house and Dave wouldn't be bothering me. Carl was usually gone to practice or a game or something, and our mother would still be in the bed.

~*~

A brief pause. I am writing this book as an adult, sneaking up on forty years old very fast. In fact, not sneaking but running. It's just around the corner. So if things are a little disjointed or out of order, it's because I am trying to write this book as I remember things, and my mind jumps around. I guess I could go back and try to put everything in chronological order, but the editor told me I don't have to do that, just write what I feel. Now of course I know that Dave was dealing in drugs, but at the age of seven, I'm not sure that I even knew what drugs were. I'm also sure that by now you will have figured out that I no longer refer to my mother as 'Mommy' or 'Mom'. I just can't relate the loving term of 'Mommy' or 'Mom' to her. There just wasn't a lot of love there, and what there was was phony. Actually, by the time I was seven, I had quit calling her by anything. I would just say as little to her as I could and try to be busy if she were awake. I have trouble at the time thinking of her as my mother because of the situation she left me in but I guess she will get what she deserves sooner or later.

~*~

Dave began to buy things for himself and for the house. He bought a new large screen television, the biggest one I had ever seen. He had a giant stereo set and lots and lots of records of all kinds. He would play loud music way into the night and sometimes the stereo played all night while he slept. He even bought me a few  things for me, mostly thin clothes and lacy underwear, which I would never wear unless he made me.

Dave also bought some dresses, shoes and  other clothes for our mother, which she wore like a proud peacock – or perhaps I should say – peahen. She would wear a new dress every weekend and would go out somewhere. She told us that she was shopping, but she almost never brought anything home.

Then my mother started going out in the afternoon. She would get out of bed about the time I would get home from school. Sometimes she would cool supper and sometimes it was Dave. When Dave did the cooking, it was almost always a pizza or some fried chicken or something else. He would just pick up the telephone and order, sometimes Chinese, but mostly pizza or chicken. I liked the pizza best, pepperoni with a lot of cheese. Dave would order anchovies and try to make me eat one, but it tasted too much like that stuff that came out of his organ when he would put it in my mouth. He would hold my nose and make me swallow that stuff and then laugh as I would run into the bathroom and vomit.

It seem that after Dave had bought our mother new clothes that she changed. She didn't work every night and some-times she didn't go to work at all. She would get out of bed about ten o'clock in the morning and lay around the house in her nightgown without even combing her hair. Sometimes she would fix lunch, but that was not very often. If I were home, I would have to scrounge around and find something to eat, most often a peanut butter and jelly sandwich. Actually, thinking back, that was probably better than what she would fix for lunch. Somehow she seemed to have lost her touch for cooking. I don't guess she really wanted cook anyway.

With her home most of the day, Dave would come and go. When some of Dave's people would come by our house, she would go out and see them. Sometimes she would come back in the house with money in her hand and put it in a drawer. Since we were really poor, I had no idea why people were giving her money, but I was smart enough to keep my mouth shut. I knew what would happen if I aggravated her and I hurt every time she would beat me. So, I just watched and kept quiet.

Then my mother started going out at night. She would dress up really nice and put on a lot of make-up and some really strong perfume. Sometimes she would hug me and Dave before she left, and sometimes she would just hug Dave, but most of the time she just went out the door without saying anything. Listening to her and Dave talking from time to time, I gathered that she was going out on a date, although I never saw anyone. She would just get in her car and leave.

Usually, she would come home sometime during the night, because when

I would get up to get ready to go to school, she would be in the bedroom, asleep and snoring. Boy, could she snore.

~*~

Dave began to tease me with his cigarettes. He started calling it his m.j. or his Mary Jane. He'd say things like, "Want a puff of my Mary Jane?" or "Want to taste something really sweet?" Or, "This m.j. will really make you feel good. Want to try some?" And of course I didn't want to do that. It seemed so nasty. But then there was Dave. He began to insist, "If you try it, I'll let you off today, and if you don't, you'll have to do double."

It didn't take many promises or threats like that to persuade me to try to smoke that strange looking cigarette. At first, I only pretended to puff on it, but then Dave hit me really hard in my belly with his fist. "Don't fool with me. I told you to smoke it. Now take a big one." And I did.

At first, it made me kind of dizzy. Sort of like my eyes couldn't focus. The same feeling I had if my head was underwater and I opened my eyes. The next thing, almost at once, was a severe pounding in my head behind my eyes. My head really hurt and I couldn't help but cry. I thought Dave was going to beat me, but he just moved over into the new leather recliner that he had purchased a couple of days earlier. He didn't say a word, just looked at me real hard. I got up and went to the bathroom where I tried to vomit, but nothing would come up. Actually, I had not had any lunch and there was nothing in my stomach. I went to bed and Dave didn't even bother to stop me, nor did he visit me that night. It was almost worth the punch and the sickness just to be left alone this night.

Of course, you know that wasn't the end of it. Dave wouldn't give up that easily and every day he made me take one or more puffs on his "Mary Jane." For a while it still made me sick, but eventually, I could smoke several puffs without becoming ill. Dave had told me that the smoke would make me 'high' but it always seemed to make me 'low'. After several days, the smoke did have some effect. After I would take a puff or two, it seemed to relax me so that I wasn't so afraid of what Dave would do to me. It also seemed to make a difference in that I didn't hurt as much while Dave was doing his thing. Finally, I got to the point that even without Dave telling me to, I would take the cigarette he was smoking and take several puffs, knowing that before the day or night was over that I would need the help. And I was right.

Even now, at my age, I am still astonished at Dave's capability to have sexual relations. From what I learned from my husband and from what I hear all the girls around me talk about, most men are satisfied with a little once in a while. Not many men can, nor do they want to, do it all the time. But Dave was always ready, always wanting to, always forcing me to. Recently I looked up a word for him, "satyr". While one definition was in Greek mythology, a half-man, half-goat, a wood-dwelling creature with the head and body of a man and the ears, horns and legs of a goat, characterized as being fond of lechery and drunken merriment could easily have fit Dave – except he didn't look like a goat, although.... – the second definition was "a man who displays inappropriate or excessive sexual behavior." Boy, did that ever fit! There may be some women who want that, but I was seven at the time, and it was much too much.

Funny, during this period of my life I don't remember much about Carl. It seems like he was there and then he was not there. I know he was at practice almost every day, and often playing a game in the afternoon or the night, but Dave never went to one. Neither did our mother, and naturally neither did I. I'm not sure what Carl knew or what he didn't know. Perhaps he knew enough to know that he really didn't want to know. You know what I mean?

~*~

For some strange reason, it seemed that after our mother quit working in the textile mill and started dating that we had more money than ever. There always seemed to be a good amount of cash money in the drawer where our mother put Dave's money. There was always something good to eat, lots of it, even if most of it was ordered from a food house or restaurant. And a lot of it was wasted as both Dave and our mother would order enough food for six or eight.

There were plenty of clothes for school or for Dave or for our mother. Even for Carl, although Carl mostly wore jeans, tennis shoes, white socks and a white t-shirt. He didn't care much for dressing up. – I wonder if he ever had a date and if he did what did he wear?

Although I had many new school clothes, Dave still insisted that I wear only a thin chemise around the house. Sometimes he would let me wear a new blouse or a t-shirt, but mostly just that stupid thin chemise. And no panties. Not ever. That was the rule. If I broke it, I would get a beating. If not from Dave, then from our mother. The only time this changed was that I was allowed to wear a sanitary belt to hold the napkin when I started my period.

One day about the middle of the morning, Dave came home looking excited. Our mother was still asleep, and he woke her up. I expected her to scream, but she just sat up in bed, her bare breast showing. She always slept nude and would only put on pajamas or a nightgown after she had got up. I waited for her to blast Dave, after all, the rule was not to disturb her while she was asleep. Evidently that didn't go for Dave.

"I found it, just like the one that we wanted." He said. She just sat there, bemused, looking at him.

"I found the house, a nice, large two-story house. Just what you wanted."

"Dave, what are you talking about?" Her voice was slurred, still sleepy, I guess.

"You know we have been talking about moving, now that we can afford it. I have been looking. And now I've found just the one we need. Four bedrooms, three or four baths, 14 rooms in all, and a large garage."

"And just where is this majestic miracle?"

"It's in Indian Trail, just off U.S. Highway 74. Trees all around. Far enough off the road to be quiet, yet close enough for....." Dave's voice trailed off as he realized that I was standing there beside the bed. "Get the hell out of here, you little sneak."

He reached out to swat me, but I was moving on his first word, realizing I had probably already most of it and not wanting to be hit yet again.

~*~

And I was right. I had heard almost all of it. Several days later, a large moving truck pulled up in our yard and several large men began loading some of our furniture in their truck.

"Leave the junky stuff here, Dave," our mother said. "Maybe the next people here will be as poor as we used to be."

"Yeah, Mom, we're only going to take the good stuff and our clothes. The rest of the garbage can just stay. The landlord has our deposit. He can use that to clean up the trailer, or he can just try to sue us."

Dave told me to get into his car, that I would be riding with him and our mother could drive her car and follow us. And that's the way we left the only home I had known.

I expected that Dave would be after me all the way along the route, but was surprised that he paid no attention to me at all. I might as well have been a basket of clothes. Now, wait a minute, I'm not complaining. As a matter of fact, I was extremely happy to just sit there, quiet as a mouse, and hope that Dave would forget all about me. Not just for that day, but forever.

And, I don't remember Carl. I suppose that he rode with our mother in her car, but for the life of me, I just can't recall. Anyway, he did move with us.

# Part 3

There were a lot of differences between our old home and our new home. The new home had a lot of land around the house, with trees almost everywhere. There wasn't much lawn, which was a good thing as Dave had no interest in mowing grass and Carl was never around, always off playing sports or practicing. And our mother certainly didn't have a "green thumb", in fact, if she ever watered a plant or tended to a flower, the plant and the flower would both die…of shock, if nothing else. That left me, and although I was a little over seven, there wasn't any way I could be a gardener.

The new house had a wide white porch that ran around on three sides, with a couple of swing seats hanging down from the porch ceiling. The house had a large living room, a formal dining room, a giant family room, another room they called a study, and then a "play room" which was the biggest room in the house. Under the stairs was a small bathroom with just a sink and a stool. Still, people called it a bathroom. Upstairs, there were four bedrooms, three of which had private bathrooms. There was one other room that Dave called a rumpus room, and a third bathroom that opened into the hallway. Biggest house I had ever seen. It seemed to be a house that would have cost a lot of money, but I knew we didn't have very much and therefore the house had to be pretty cheap or we couldn't afford it. Still, my mind told me that

Dave and our mother was getting money from somewhere and perhaps they were getting enough to pay for this house. Anyway, I had my own room – although Dave removed the lock so I couldn't lock him out – and so did Dave and Carl. Our mother took the largest room with the biggest bath, but what else could you expect.

There were a lot of nooks and crannies as the home was a Victorian style two-story with bay windows and turrets. There was also a large storage room under the stairway leading to the second floor. Dave built some shelves and racks in that storage room and that's where he stored his stuff. You know, the stuff that he was selling. Now when someone came to the house, he would have them wait in the living room while he took whatever they were buying out of his stash under the stairwell.

Dave also built a large storage box in the walk-in closet in his room. He didn't hang clothes in that closet, at least not very many. Most of the closet was taken up by that storage box. Over a period of time, I learned that is where he stored the money that he would receive from his people. I also learned that I would get the beating of my life if I ever touched that box, much less any of the money stored there. Only Dave or our mother was allowed to go into that closet. In fact, Dave promised to beat me if I even went into his room, so I stayed away.

One day Dave came home driving a bright read new car. I thought it was beautiful, but Dave wouldn't let me ride in it. Not at first, anyway. He just parked the car under the trees where the birds would drop stuff on the car and then I would have to clean the car anytime that Dave wanted to drive it.

The only thing good about the new house was that Dave left me alone. At least, at first. However after several weeks it became the same old thing, only now Dave would have to be serviced before I went to school, so he would wake me up early so that I could take care of him and still catch the school bus. Then, when I came home from school, it was time to service him again. Most of the time, that took care of him, but sometimes he would come into my room after I was in bed and do it again.

Carl was still away most of the time, coming home only to eat and sleep. There were times that he didn't even come home at night. Sometimes he was playing sports somewhere that he had to stay overnight. The rest of the nights away were probably with some girl. I told you that Carl was quite attractive and very popular. I just know that a lot of girls must have found that attractive.

By now, any time that Dave was after me, he would give me puffs off his cigarette, and of course, over time it got to where I would always take those puffs. It seemed to make things easier. At least, I could stand it when Dave did his thing, and then forget about him as soon as he had finished and I could go wash myself. I had tried for a while not to bathe every day hoping that the smell would turn him off, but it seemed to have the opposite effect, so I made sure to wash after ever time and to take a full bath every day. At least my body was clean, if not my soul.

There was a time when I was about nine that I noticed that Dave wasn't around for a while. I don't know where he went and bluntly I didn't care. I was just glad that he was gone. No, I didn't ask my mother and certainly she didn't bother to tell me. Still, that was just fine with me.

Then, one day, Dave drove up in the yard with his red car. I had been so happy that he was gone I didn't even notice that his car was gone too. Anyway, he drove up in the yard and got out, carrying two large suitcases. He brought them in the house and went straight to his storage room under the stairway. I believe I forgot to tell you that he had put locks on the door to the storage room and he had to use a key to open the door. I think I remember that there were two keys and that our mother had the second one.

Of course you know what happened after that. It seemed that Dave intended to make up on all that he had missed while he was absent, so it was morning, afternoon and night. I got so sore that I could hardly walk, and even my teacher noticed something as she asked if I was alright, if my legs were hurting me. I told her that I had played too much and that the muscles were sore but that I was okay. She seemed to accept that without asking any more questions.

It was only a couple of days later that Dave did something different. I had come home from school, and of course I had to do my "job". After Dave finished, it seemed that he was in a pretty good mood. He said that he had something special for me. That scared me because every time he had something for me, it always turned out to be the same thing. Or most of the time, it was something even worse. Still, I knew that if I didn't accept whatever it was that he had, I would just get another beating.

Another pause. When I say beating, I don't mean just a beating. I mean a BEATING. Whether it was our mother or Dave that gave it to me, a beating meant that blood would flow. Using a switch or a belt, whichever was handy, Dave or our mother would make me take off my clothes and whip me across my back and buttocks. They knew that if I showed up at school with marks and scars that could be seen, they would be in big trouble with the authorities, so the whipped me where my clothes would hide the damage. And there was always damage. Many nights I would wake up and find blood on my sheets and there was always blood after their beating.

As I was saying, Dave told me that he had something special for me. I didn't ask what it was, knowing that he would tell me when he wanted me to know. So I just sat there. Dave put out his hand and between his fingers there was a little red pill. "Here – take it. It'll make you feel good."

I didn't believe Dave, he had never given me anything that made me feel good..although the mary jane he had me smoke made things seem to be a little better. "That is one of the small ones, only a 60," he said.

*Sixty what?* I didn't know what he was talking about at the time. Anyway, with him glaring at me with his angry eyes, I took the pill from him. "Now take it," he said. "No, take it here," as I started to get off his bed. He reached out and got a bottle of beer that had been sitting on the night table and gave it to me. He watched me every second, so I knew that I would have to take the pill, and take it with beer, which I hated. But I hated being beaten even more, so I swallowed the pill with the beer. For a moment, I thought I was going to throw up all over him. *Serve him right, making me drink that stupid beer.* The moment of nausea passed, and gave him the bottle back. "Now just sit there a few minutes. I promise you will feel better."

What choice did I have? Of course, I sat there and waited. But then I began to feel a little different. I wasn't hurting as much where Dave had done his thing, in fact, I wasn't hurting much of anywhere, as a feeling spread all over me. Even my mind seemed to ease up and I wasn't afraid of Dave any more.

He could evidently see the difference because he began to laugh. "I see that you are beginning to feel it," he said. "I told you it would make it feel good."

And he was right. It was making me feel good. In fact, it was making me feel real good, even great, even happy; so happy in fact that I reached out and hugged Dave and even kissed him, something I don't remember having ever done. It made me feel so good that I wanted to do something for Dave, and of course you know what Dave wanted. And that night he got it. No, the sex didn't feel good; in fact I didn't feel anything at all. But let me tell you, that little red pill certainly made me feel fantastic.

The next day when I got home from school, I was hoping that Dave would give me another one of those pills before he started on me. But he didn't. And I knew better than to ask him for one. That would just make him mad, then he would beat me and make sure that I never got another one. So, I just made do with several puffs off his 'mary jane', but it just wasn't the same. The pain was there and seemed to be even worse this time. Now I realize it seemed that way because there was no relief, there was no little red pill to dull the pain.

~*~

Patricia Ann Browne

Over the next several weeks, or
months, nothing seemed to change very
much. Our mother would get a call during the
afternoon or evening. She would dress up
and then go out, sometimes not getting back
home until the next day. Then she would
sleep until after lunch. It seemed like she
never cooked any more, if there was food it
was Dave or me. Yes, me. I was getting close
to ten years old so more and more often if I
wanted anything to eat I would have to make
it. I soon got tired of banana sandwiches or
baloney sandwiches or even peanut butter
and jelly sandwiches, so I learned to cook
eggs. Mostly scrambled because I just
couldn't learn to open the egg without
breaking the yoke, but that was okay because
I like my eggs all mixed up. Dave wouldn't
eat anything that I cooked, I guess he was
scared I'd poison him. Anyway, it seemed
that he never ate, or at least not very much.
He was just walking around with a cigarette

in his mouth, and now it wasn't 'mary jane' it was just a cigarette. Still, it seemed that he was always just a little bit out of it, like he was when he first started smoking 'm.j.' Several times I saw him take a pill which I don't believe was aspirin. He was in too good a mood. Even so, he didn't let up on me, making me do it two and sometimes three times a day.

Dave still had a lot of people come see him, only now some of them would sit in the living room with him, talking for much of the night. A lot of them would smoke 'mary jane', I could tell because the smell was all over the house. I was not allowed to go into the living room, in fact, I was not allowed to meet or even see the people who visited Dave. I do know that whatever they came to get, Dave had in his storage room under the stairwell, and when the people would leave, Dave would go into his room and close the door. While I couldn't see it, I could hear him open his closet and put something in the storage box. Money that he got from the people, I guess.

~*~

Then Dave changed. He started having me bring beer and drinks into the living room while people were there. There were a lot of different people who came, some men and some women. Some were not very old and others were much older, even with white hair. Dave would ask them what they wanted to drink. We had beer, Budweiser Light and regular Budweiser (Not an endorsement, I hated that stuff, and still do) as well as Coke and diet Coke. Most of the people wanted beer, but a few wanted something else either soda pop or water. Some of them said they didn't want to get stopped by the police on their way home. (Yeah, now I realize it. What if they had a little too much to drink and were stopped by the police. With whatever they would have in their car, they would probably go to jail. That never happened, darn it!)

Anyway, now I was able to see the people who came to see Dave. They all seemed to be just people, but some of them seemed sleepy or tired. I wondered why they just didn't go home and go to bed. Some of the others seemed to be very excited, almost jumping around like Mexican beans. The rest of them were just people, just sitting and talking, although one of the old men would joke with me when I served him his Coke. He had short hair that was completely white, although there wasn't much there. His face was round, and so was his stomach. I bet he played Santa at Christmas. Still, I knew that Dave didn't want me talking to anyone. He was afraid I would say something that might get him in trouble, so I would just serve the drinks and then go back to my room until Dave called me again. Sometimes I would have to serve drinks two or three times during the night. You might think that after that Dave would be too tired to do anything that night, but you would be wrong. I can't explain it, he seemed be always ready and for some reason he didn't have a girl friend to do it with; only me.

~*~

It became an every night thing. Dave would have a lot of people that would come by and spend time at our house, and I would always be the maid. Sometimes I would have to make sandwiches for everybody, and always I would have to serve drinks. I think most of the people either got used to seeing me or just ignored me, which was just fine. There was one, the old man with the white hair, that seemed to always be there. He would come over every night. I never saw him smoke anything or take anything except for the soft drink, and it was always the same: Coca Cola. He would take the glass, make a joke or two and then pat me on my arm. He always had something nice to say, and his jokes weren't really funny, but they seemed to make him happy, so I tried to laugh. That would make him smile at me.

Dave didn't seem to mind when the old man would talk to me, so I would stand close to him so that I could hear above the noise of the rest of the people. There were usually ten or fifteen people, and when that many people are smoking, drinking and talking in one room, the noise makes it hard to hear. But the old man was patient with me, repeating anything that I didn't hear. He would always pat my arm when I served him, but otherwise didn't touch me. He was nice, saying that I was good-looking (hah) and that I was a good little girl for listening to an old man talk. I didn't mind, in fact I liked to listen to him since he wasn't mad, or drunk, and he didn't yell at me, like some of the others did if I was too slow serving them their drinks and sandwiches. I tried to be as fast as possible because I knew that if Dave's people were unhappy I would get another beating. It had happened all too often, so I would run between the living room and the kitchen, trying to be even faster.

~*~

One night it was different. Dave came over to the old man while I was standing by him, waiting for him to empty his glass so I could get him another Coke. Dave asked the old man if he liked what he saw. The old man stuttered and stammered. "Well?" Dave asked him. I didn't hear what the old man said. Dave turned to me and told me to go serve the others. I went, but kept looking back to where Dave and the old man were. They were doing lot of talking and it was the first time I saw Dave even speak with the old man.

After everybody left, Dave told me to go up to my room and wait for him, that he would be up there shortly. I knew what he meant when he said for me to wait for him, so I took off all my clothes and laid down on the bed to wait for Dave. It seemed that he was especially eager that night and it took a long time for him to get everything that he wanted and then he left me alone.

The next morning after I finished with Dave and I was putting my clothes on to go to school, Dave told me that he was going to give me something special for my tenth birthday. It wasn't far away, but from the "surprises" I had received from Dave for my other birthdays, I was really afraid. I wished for my birthday to go away because the "surprises" were never pleasant, just more of the same thing.

Still, my tenth birthday did arrive. There was no cake or anything as our mother was never there in the evenings. She was always going out to meet whoever it was that called her. I didn't find out until much later what she was doing while she was gone. I guess that explained a lot about the money we always seemed to have now, but at the time I didn't think too much about it because there was always Dave, and now there was a bunch of people in our house almost every night. The people kept changing, some would leave and others would come in to take their place. But the old man was there every night and he was usually the last one to leave. He and Dave would talk a lot out on the porch before he left.

Anyhow, it was my tenth birthday and I didn't have a cake and our mother never bothered to buy me a present. In fact, I couldn't remember the last time she had ever bought me a present of any kind. At one time she never had the money and once she began having money, she didn't bother. I was worried that day because Dave had promised me something special and I was afraid it would be something bad. Still, while I was working on him that morning before school, he didn't say a word, not even when I went outside to wait for the school bus. I believed that he had forgotten about it and I really hoped that he had forgotten. But Dave almost never forgot anything.

After school, it was the same thing again, and then it was time to get ready for the people to start arriving. I made a bunch of sandwiches, mostly ham and cheese, but also a peanut butter and jelly sandwich which I sat aside for the old man. I knew he would be there and I knew that he liked my sandwiches, using a smooth type peanut butter and grape jelly. He always had one with his Coke. I was sure to put a good coating of peanut butter and a lot of grape jelly, because that was the way he seemed to like it.

That night there seemed to be even more people than normal. I was kept busy running between the kitchen and the living room, but I could see Dave go over to the old man several times and they would talk for a while and then Dave would move on. I would wait for Dave to leave before I would take the Coke and sandwich to the old man. I was hoping he would say something about what he and Dave were talking about, but he never said a word, just telling me a joke or two, most of which he had already told me several times, but I didn't mind since it made him smile at me a lot.

The party – if that was what it was – seemed to last longer that night, but eventually the people started leaving. Dave told me to go up to my room and I would find a surprise waiting for me. I didn't have the slightest idea what it was but dared not disobey Dave. I knew what would happen if I did. When I got to my room, I found a box on my bed. I opened the box and inside was a frilly black nightgown that was so thin you could see through it. I knew what was coming, or at least I thought I did. I knew that I had to put on that nightgown and that Dave would soon be up there. Sure enough, in just a little while, Dave came into my room, but this time he wasn't alone. The old man with white hair was with him.

"Here's another surprise," Dave said, holding out his hand. I could see that he had one of the little red pills that had made me feel so good. I had a glass of water on the night table close to my bed, so I took the pill and swallowed it right away. I was looking forward to the feeling that it caused, but I was wondering why the old man was there. Still, with Dave, I didn't dare ask a lot of questions, because he would hit me or beat me, so I just waited. In just a few minutes, I began to feel like I was floating, the feeling good had started again. Dave looked me but I couldn't focus on him, his nose seemed to grow a lot. Dave stood up, turned to the old man and said that it was okay now. I didn't know what that meant, but I was soon to find out. Dave left my room and closed the door behind him, leaving me alone with the old man.

He came over to where I was sitting on my bed and patted my arm and then my shoulder, leaving his hand on my shoulder for a long time. That didn't bother me, this was the only person who had been friendly to me and if he wanted to pat me, that would be alright. It was just feeling good...no, not good. Great. Better and better.

You can probably guess what happened next. The old man continued to pat me and caress me and it wasn't long until he was in the bed with me. I didn't care, I was feeling too good. I let him do anything he wanted to, at least this wasn't Dave. I didn't really feel anything at all, no pain or anything. I was just floating on my cloud that the little red pill gave me. The old man finished, got out of bed and put his clothes back on. He looked at me like he wanted to say something. I thought he was going to apologize, but I just smiled at him. It was okay. Then he left. But Dave hadn't got his and it was only minutes until he came back into my room and got on my bed. I was still feeling fantastic, so I guess I was cooperative. Still floating, I didn't feel pain like I did most of the time. In fact, I actually went to sleep before Dave finished.

~*~

After that night, it wasn't long until Dave left me with another man. This time the man wasn't the nice old man but a rough younger man. Still, the little red pill that Dave gave me each time made me feel so good, I didn't really care who was there. It became an almost every night thing. Usually it was always men but sometimes it would be a woman. And sometimes both a man and a woman. I didn't care, the little red pill took care of everything.

Sometimes afterwards, it seemed that I had to have a pill every night. I would do anything that Dave wanted me to as long as he would give me a pill. There were nights when he wouldn't give me a pill until I begged him to, and if he wanted to punish me, he certainly knew how. He would just withhold the pill and I would suffer more than from a beating.

One night after I had finished serving the first group of people their drinks and sandwiches, I went up to my room to use the bathroom. Knowing that Dave was with the people downstairs, I sneaked into his room. There on the bureau there were several of the little red pills. I took two, believing that perhaps he wouldn't miss only two, and took them into my room where I hid them in the pocket of one of my coats hanging in the closet. I didn't dare use one at that time because I knew that Dave would be able to tell by looking at me. So, I just went back downstairs, secure in the knowledge that I had a secret stash in case he didn't give me my nightly dose. I should have known better.

Dave must have kept count of every one of those pills. After everyone had left and I went to my room to wait for whatever would happen, I could hear Dave in his room. Then the door to my room opened and Dave walked in with a sinister grin on his face. *Oh Oh.* I could tell from the look on his face that he knew I had taken some of his pills. He came over to the bed, grabbed me by the arm and yanked me out onto the floor.

Sitting down on the bed, he grabbed me again and pulled me upside down across his knees. "I'll teach you not to steal from me." He tore the new nightgown off me, not even bothering to untie the belt. Then he began to spank me on my bare bottom. That hurt. I told you he has big hands and the slap, slap, slap of that large hand on my bare flesh echoed throughout the room. And it didn't stop. I thought it would never stop. But then, Dave stopped spanking me, just letting his had rest on by butt. Although I was sobbing, I felt a little relief that the spanking had stopped. But there was something worse in store. "I told you I'd teach you not to steal from me." He put me face down on my bed and crawled between my legs. *Oh my God! The pain!* Everything went black.

# Part 4

Oxycodone. That was the little red pill that Dave was giving to me. If you had asked me the name, I would have never known, not at the age of ten. But I have looked it up and I know why I would feel so good after taking one. Taking one that Dave gave me, that is. He did indeed teach me not to steal from him and I never did again. It seemed that I didn't have to, because Dave almost never again refused to give me one each night. He evidently figured it out that it would keep me tame and under his control and he liked it that way.

He used to take the pill also, although he had a lot of other stuff he would use. I didn't know what they were and he would never give me anything except for the little pill or sometimes he would give me a hand-rolled cigarette, but I didn't really like the taste of the smoke and 'mary jane' or, as I found out, marijuana just didn't have the same effect as the little red pill. It was okay, it just didn't do the job.

The people kept coming to our house, it seems like there was a party every night. The only thing is that the kind old man no longer came to our house. I was sorry about that, I missed him.

The nightly visits to my room by different men and some women continued, but seemed to ease off as it wasn't every night and sometimes not even one time a week. That was just peachy keen with me, so long as the little red pills continued to roll in, and Dave made sure they did. I found out later that there were different grades of the oxycodone, a 60 milligram pill that Dave was giving to me and others as high as 160 milligrams, but he never gave me one that strong. It turned out that the stuff he was selling came mostly from Canada, as it was stronger than what was available as an average in the United States.

Dave seemed to be changing. It was like he was almost always taking pills or powder or something because he would be unsteady and times wasn't even able to walk straight. It didn't seem to affect his mind, as he never forgot anything that I did, nor did it slow down his sex drive. I can't say that it made it any worse but I can say it didn't slow it down any.

After my tenth birthday, there were many times that I would come home from school and find the house empty. There were a few times that Carl might be there and other times our mother might be, but more and more often Dave would not be at home when I got there. Hey, not that I'm complaining, in fact quite the opposite. The only trouble was that eventually he would come back, speeding his car into the yard and sliding to a stop that would almost hit a tree or the porch. I'm not sure if that was because he was taking the drugs that he used or if it was because he was in a hurry to get home to me. For sure, he was at me almost as soon as the front door closed. I got to the point that if Dave wasn't home I would still go to my room, take off my school clothes and put on one of the chemises that Dave had bought me. I knew it was only a matter of time before he would be there and I had better be ready. Otherwise, there would be a beating and still he would go ahead and do his thing with me.

I was so numb that I couldn't even think about running away from home. I knew if I even attempted to do so that Dave would find me. Or our mother would find me. If I did run away, I would be found by the police and returned home and that would lead to either Dave or our mother – or sometimes both – beating me yet again. I could only pray for some relief, but with what I was going through, it is understandable if I really didn't think that God was going to intervene. And he – or she – didn't. Or so I thought.

One evening just before I was eleven years old, I was sitting on my bed, in my chemise, waiting for the inevitable. I didn't dare to not be ready when Dave got home. A strange car pulled up in our yard. It was a police car from the nearby town, and a policeman got out. I recognized it as a police car because I had seen it on display at our school one time when a police woman had come to our school to talk about crime. I was home by myself so I quickly put on my dress and ran downstairs. The policeman was knocking on the door. Dave had disconnected the doorbell because he didn't want all his people ringing the doorbell all the time. I opened the door and a man in a police uniform stood there.

"Is your father or your mother home?"

"My father is dead."

"Is your mother home?"

"No."

"Is there anyone home with you?"

"No, I'm here by myself."

"How old are you?"

"Almost eleven."

"And they left you here alone?"

"I'm a big girl, I can take care of myself."

"Well, maybe. But they shouldn't leave you here alone."

"Do you want something." I knew that if he wanted some of the stuff that Dave sold I couldn't give it to him because Dave always kept his storage room locked.

"Are you related to Dave Browne?"

"Yes, I'm his sister."

"Is your mother coming home soon."

"Probably, but sometimes she stays out all night."

"What is your name?"

"My name is Patricia Ann Browne. What's yours?"

"I'm Deputy Wilson. I'm from the Sheriff's department."

"So what do you want?" (Average kid's straight question)

"Tell your mother to get in touch with the Sheriff's office when she comes home."

"Is there something wrong? You asked about Dave. Is he in trouble?"

"No, he's not in trouble. He was killed in a car accident tonight."

"Dave got killed?"

"Yes, little girl…er..Patricia. Have your mother call us."

"Dave is dead?"

"Uh-huh. Just have your mother give us a call."

"Okay."


I shut the door and climbed the stairs. Inside my room I took off my dress and sat on the side of my bed for a long time. Then it soaked in. *Dave is dead. Dave is dead. Dave is Dead. Dave is **DEAD**! There is a God.* I rose up out of my bed, took off my chemise so that I was naked. I went to the closet and took one of the little red pills out of my coat pocket where they had been since I first stole them from Dave. I took the glass of water and swallowed one of the pills. Then I just lay back on my bed, humming over and over, "Dave is dead, Dave is dead," and let the good feeling take me away again, this time without any pain.

~*~

Our mother didn't get home until almost ten o'clock the next morning. Carl had not come home and our mother had spent the night away, probably with one of her many men friends that seemed to like to give her money and stuff. At first she didn't seem to notice but then she looked surprised that I was still at home and not in school.

"Are you sick?"
"No."
"Didn't you go to school?"
"No."
"Why not?"
"I just didn't go."

"Does Dave know that you skipped school?"

"No."

"Why not? Didn't you tell him?"

"No."

"Why not?"

"I couldn't."

"Why not?"

"He wasn't here."

"Where is he?"

"I don't know."

"Why not?"

"He's dead."

"He's what?"

"He is dead. Dave is dead." I guess that I must have sounded too happy because she slapped me hard enough to make my nose bleed.

"What the hell are you saying, you snotty-nosed brat? What do you mean Dave's dead?"

"He's dead. The policeman said he's dead."

"What policeman?"

You will notice about this time we are not having the greatest of time conversing. I'm ashamed to admit it, but I was having fun teasing her.

"A policeman came last night. He told me to tell you that Dave is dead and that you are to call the sheriff's department and that Dave was in an accident and that Dave is dead." I got all that out in one breath.

She fainted. Just flopped over.

I didn't know what to do, so I didn't do anything. I just left here lying there on the floor. I went into the kitchen to make myself a peanut and butter sandwich. It seemed like the thing do.

After what seemed to be a long time, I heard her shrill voice on the telephone, "What do you mean my son is dead?" Then it went quiet before she said, in a different voice, "I'll be there in a little while."

I sat at the table, eating my sandwich and drinking a glass of milk, while my mother went into her room, put on some different clothes and then she left without saying a word to me. I could hear her car really take off as she left the yard. I just finished my milk and sandwich and then went upstairs. I had something special on my mind.

If Dave was really dead, he would have no use for the little red pills he kept in his room, and I was going to get them. Turns out there were a couple of bottles of the pills in the room along with several bottles of other stuff, so I just took everything into my room and hid them among my clothes. Then another thought struck me. I went back into Dave's room and for the first time opened the storage box he had built into his closet. It was literally crammed full of money, more money than I had ever seen in my life. It looked like every one of them were one hundred dollar bills and I bet there were a billion of them. Well, maybe not a billion, but a lot. and that was a big box, taking up most of the closet. I knew it was money that Dave and our mother had put in there and I was certain that if I took some, no one would ever know. I went back downstairs and into the kitchen, where I took a large garbage bag out of the pantry and went back upstairs. I filled the bag with money until it was almost too heavy for me to pick up, but there were still scads of money in the box. I took the bag into my room, where I pushed it under my bed. I knew that my mother had almost never been into my room and I didn't believe that anyone would ever find out that I had taken some of the money. *Anyway,* I reasoned, *I think I've earned what I'm taking..*

Turned out that it was true. Dave was dead, sure enough. And our mother was really grief-stricken. We had all known that he was her favorite and that she had loved him most. It wasn't until I was going through her estate papers later that I found out that she did indeed love him, and not just as a son. Evidently just using me wasn't enough for Dave; he had to have even more. Even his own mother.

Carl came home for Dave's funeral. He was a junior in college, having won a partial scholarship for playing football. Between Dave and our mother, there was enough money to pay the rest of his tuition and living expenses, so Carl had decided to go to college in West Virginia.

Carl still had his room in our house and that is where he stayed while he was home. He didn't seem too gloomy about Dave's death, nowhere near as grieving as our mother, but then I found out that Carl really didn't like his brother all that much. Especially as he knew about the drugs and the people. Still, Carl didn't seem to know about what Dave was doing to me, and he didn't know what Dave was having other people do to me. I think that I was still Carl's little sister in his eyes, and the fact that I was right at eleven years old didn't make that any different. He would hug me when he came close; a warm, friendly hug that wasn't at all like the aggressive, grabbing, possessive hug that I would get from Dave.

Carl didn't hang around our mother very much and it didn't seem to matter to her. But I liked it and in fact when went to the funeral he held my arm while some strange man was escorting our mother. I don't know who he was because I had never seen him before, nor have I seen him since.

The funeral was on a Saturday afternoon and Carl was going to return to his college on Sunday afternoon, but he would stay with us on Saturday night. As usual, our mother, all dressed up, went out again on that night. It didn't seem that she missed Dave at all, or at least she wasn't going to take any time off if she did. But, she did miss one thing. That was the key to Dave's car, which the sheriff's deputy gave to me. Unknown to my mother, on the same key ring was a key to our house and more importantly, a key to Dave's storage room under the stairway. The only person other than me that knew was Carl and that was only because I let him pick up some of the stuff that Dave kept locked up. Carl only took a small bag full, mostly just marijuana. He was never into drugs much because of wanting to play sports. Then I locked the storage room again and hid the keys in my room.

After raiding Dave's stash, Carl and I were sitting the kitchen, not talking, just sitting there. I don't think either one of us especially missed Dave; Carl because he wasn't that close to his older brother – or half-brother as it turned out. What really happened was that Dave's father was our mother's brother, Carl's father was another man who had married our mother but only lived with her for a year or so. Then there was my father; he was the one killed in the accident. That meant that Dave and Carl and I were all just half-brothers and half-sisters, if you get my drift. Guess our mother was busy.

Anyway, as I sat there in the kitchen with Carl, I knew that I certainly wouldn't miss the abuse that I had suffered. I suppose that I was even a little giddy. I had made Carl my favorite, what I call my specialty, a peanut butter and jelly sandwich, with a glass of cold milk. Carl was like me, he didn't at all care for the taste of beer.

After eating the sandwich, I went upstairs to my room. Carl stayed below and actually cleaned up the kitchen. I liked that because almost all of the time I was the one who had to do the cleaning, and it was a joy to let someone else do it for a change.

Knowing that Dave could no longer bother me, I didn't hesitate. I knew that I had a second pill in my coat pocket, you know, the ones I stole first that got my spanking and the after effect. As soon as I got to my room, I took that pill out of my pocket and swallowed it. I knew it would make me feel good, and I was ready. I undressed, not bothering to put on a chemise or nightgown and lay down on my bed. It felt just great. Hum…*Dave is dead. I got a pill. All is right with the world.*

Just about the time that the pill
took effect, my door opened. At first, I
was terrified, forgetting for a second that
Dave was dead, and then Carl stuck his
head inside. "You okay, sis? Thought I
heard a noise."

"Probably just me laughing. Or
maybe I was cheering." I'm not sure if I
actually said that out loud or if I just
thought it in my mind. Anyway, Carl
came the rest of the way into my room.
"Are you okay, Patty?" This time I know
I answered. "I'm just fine. I feel great."

Carl came closer to my bed where
I was now lying on by back, looking up
at the ceiling, admiring all of the colorful
rainbows and clouds that had appeared.
He looked at my face and eyes, and then

laughed a little. "Yes, I guess you do feel good. At least, you look like you're feeling good."

"It's just a little something that Dave taught me," I said. "Some little something that will just make you feel great. Want some?"

"No, I don't think so."

"It'll make you feel good. Good like me." I sat up, paying no attention to the fact that I wasn't wearing any clothes, and hugged Carl. "Don't you want to feel good?"

Carl hugged me back. "I feel pretty good anyway. In fact, now I feel really good. You know, you're pretty. I bet when you grow up you'll be beautiful, probably break a lot of hearts."

"I'm a big girl now."

"Yeah, sure you are. A big girl of eleven. You're still just a kid."

For some reason, that aggravated me. I knew from past experience what to do to a man, so I reached up and grabbed Carl by the hair and brought his mouth to mine. At first, there was some resistance but that quickly faded. And you know what came next. Truth of it is that I didn't feel anything. Nothing good, nothing bad, just nothing.

I suppose if I wanted to, I could blame it on the little red pills, or I could blame it on loneliness, or that I wanted to make Carl feel good. The thing is that the only way I knew to reward Carl for caring for me was to do what we did. After all, it wasn't something new and it didn't hurt. Not then.

The next morning Carl wouldn't even face me. He refused to eat the peanut butter and jelly sandwich that I made for him although I used his favorite crunchy peanut butter and his favorite jelly, apricot. In fact, as soon as he woke up and showered, he put on his clothes and then he took off, driving the beat-up old car that Dave had passed along to him after he got his new red car. Carl had driven the car to college, but most of the time it just sat around, and Carl didn't party much and the transportation to practice and the games was furnished by the school.

Carl didn't even wait until the afternoon to leave. I was hurt. Carl didn't even say goodbye. I was alone.

But not for long. That same night, people would knock on our door. It was some of the same bunch of people that would come by and see Dave. It didn't take much to realize that as long as there was stuff in the storage room under the stairwell that I would continue to have visitors. The only down thing was that eventually the hoard had been used up. During the next few weeks, I received a lot of money for the stuff. The fact was that I didn't know how much to charge for that stuff, but the people were most helpful in telling me the prices. I don't believe they cheated me too much because I received a lot of money, a whole lot of money.

Still, the time came when the storage room was finally empty – except for the stuff that I kept for myself – and I didn't know where to go to get any more. As the supply dwindled, so did the visitors and finally all of the supplies had been sold and there were no more visitors except that once in a while someone would stop by to see if I had anything left. Unfortunately I didn't. Unfortunate, because if I had been able to find more, I could have made a fortune. But, that's life. I would have to be satisfied with what I had received. When I finally got around to counting the money, including the sack that I had hidden under my bed, I had possession of over one million, two hundred thousand dollars. I was a rich woman. Or at least, I was a rich eleven-year old. And pregnant.

# Part 5

During the two months that it took me to sell all of the drugs that Dave had stored under the stairwell, I very rarely even saw our mother. She would get out of bed in the middle of the afternoon, fix herself a snack and wait for a telephone call, which inevitably came. Then she would dress up in sexy clothes, a lot of make-up and a lot of perfume and leave. She wouldn't even take the trouble to tell me she was leaving and of course she never said goodbye. That was just fine with me. To say that I hated her for letting Dave do the things to me that he did is a slight understatement. My only thought was that it was too bad that it wasn't her that was driving the car when Dave was killed. Maybe God would have seen fit to call them both home, if indeed that was their final destination. I still have trouble believing that Dave will be on a cloud somewhere in heaven. But that will be as it is. No, I don't forgive him. I just don't think about him at all. Until I started this book, I thought I had shut him out of my mind for good.

Anyway, so there we were; one mother who wasn't really a mother and one little girl who wasn't really a little girl. No way anyone can remain a little girl and go through everything that I had experienced. One thing I did have was a lot of money. More money than most people have all their lives. Only I didn't know what to do with it. I knew if I buried it that it would get wet and rot. Then it would be no good. I knew that I couldn't put it in the bank, because I was too young to open a bank account. I also knew that if I kept it in my room, sooner or later someone might find out. Then, I would lose it.

So I did what I thought was best. I hid it. What I actually did was that I separated the money into different piles. Then I put each pile into a plastic garbage bag and then put that garbage bag into a second and then into a third garbage bag. Then I took a piece of rope and climbed up in the trees that com-pletely surrounded the house. I put one bag full of money into one tree and the other bags into other trees, climbing as high as I dared. I was hoping that if anyone noticed the bag it would be taken as a squirrel's nest – there were a lot of them in the tree branches – or perhaps a bunch of old leaves. It must have worked because no one ever found the bags until I was able to get them when I was older.

Even at the ripe old age of eleven years, I knew that I had to remain in school or the authorities would come get me. I didn't want to take a chance so I began to ride the bus to school every morning and then back home every afternoon. I began to study once again and my grades began to rise. But there was something else that was rising. My belly. It continued to grow. I couldn't understand why, but my clothes were getting tighter. I rationalized that it was because I was getting older.

Thinking back, with all of the stuff that I went through with Dave and the men that he gave me to, it is a miracle that I never became pregnant. There was no such thing as protected sex. Not from those beasts. Perhaps it was because I was so young that I couldn't conceive. However, I have read about girls becoming pregnant before they were ten. Most of them were from some tribe or another so it is possible that Caucasians mature later and that might what prevented me from conceiving. Now, all of a sudden, I was getting sick in the morning, often too sick to even go to school, I would vomit until there was nothing left, but I was still getting bigger.

I was now in the sixth grade at school and had heard a lot of talk about boys and girls, about babies and sexual acts. *Could I be pregnant? Nah!* But I kept growing.

One afternoon after school, I had stopped by a convenience store to pick up a six-pack of Cokes. I had always kept some available, just in case that old man with white hair ever came back to visit. I had even gotten to where I enjoyed the taste of Coca Cola. I didn't mind the caffeine and I was somewhat under-weight, so the sugar wouldn't hurt me. The storekeeper looked at me kind of funny and then said, "Little girl, you're not pregnant, are you?"

Of course, I denied that I was, but I wasn't exactly sure of what pregnancy was. One good thing was that Dave had bought a good computer before he died, one of the top on the market, and I knew how to use it. When I had researched the Internet and read all I could about pregnancy, I became frightened, certain that I was pregnant. *Barely eleven and I'm pregnant? I'm going to have a baby?* No way. I couldn't do that. I couldn't bring a baby in the world. *How could I take care of it? What would I do?* And then another thought, *who can I tell?* And then it hit me, **Carl.** In fact, I must have been blind…or dumb…or both. It had to be Carl. The one time we did it must have been it. I hadn't had sex with anyone for several weeks before Carl, and now I was pregnant. According to the information on the internet, I was probably only a couple of months along, and there were other articles about abortion. I wasn't exactly sure how to go about that even though there were a lot of stories about people who had done it themselves. That scared me even more, but it seemed to be the perfect solution to my problem, if only I could find an adult that I could trust. It couldn't be my mother. It couldn't be my teacher. There was no one else, it had to be Carl. So I called him.

Carl had left a telephone number at the college where we could call him, but he didn't answer the telephone when I called. I left a message with his roommate, a dumb sounding boy who just tried to flirt with me. Carl did call back that same night. I told him that I had to see him, had to talk with him. He told me that he couldn't just leave, that he had classes. What was my problem? I couldn't tell him on the telephone I could only ask him if he remembered the last night at home. He said he did, and then I told him that something had happened and I needed to see him right away. I think he may have gotten the idea so he said he would come down over the weekend and see me. I didn't want our mother to know what was happening, and although she was rarely home, I asked Carl to meet me at the McDonalds. I knew we would be safe meeting there because our mother would not be caught dead eating in McDonalds. Not enough class, she would say.

Carl got to the McDonalds around seven o'clock on Saturday evening. I had been waiting since four-thirty, ordering drink after drink so that I wouldn't be asked to leave. I was almost beginning to believe that Carl wasn't coming. It would be just like a man. But then he showed up, sliding in the booth across from me, and asking, "What's the problem, sis?"

"I'm pregnant," I blurted. A look of shock came across Carl's face, causing it to become beet red. He stuttered and stammered, asking if I was sure, and if I was certain that it had happened because of what had taken place between us. I told him everything, all about what Dave had done and about the men and the women and the drugs. I told him that the only person that could have caused me to get pregnant was him, as no one else had touched me for weeks. I believe it finally soaked in.

"What can we do?" he asked. I believe that he was even more upset and confused than I was when I first found out.

"I just can't have a baby at eleven." I said. Then I told him about the possibility of an abortion. He didn't like the idea, thinking that it might cause me a lot of harm. I told him everything that I had read, about how abortion wasn't particularly dangerous if it were done in the first few months, but as time would go by, it would become more dangerous. I told him that I had read about women using a coat hanger that would cause an abortion, and that was what I was going to do, with him or without him. I thought he was going to faint.

"Carl, the only thing you have to do is to be at the house in case some happens. Then you can take me to the hospital. Okay?"

You would not believe the reluctance he showed. He was definitely against any abortion, he was sure it was murder, killing a baby. But he didn't have any way of explaining how an eleven-year-old girl could become pregnant. And if tests were taken, it might show him up as the father. We argued for a long time. It was only after I convinced him that I was going to do it any way that he finally agreed. He would come to the house and after we made sure that our mother was not there, he would

151

stay downstairs and I would do what was necessary. If there was any problem, he would be able to get a doctor or take me to get medical attention. And that is the way it was done.

What they didn't mention on the internet was the amount of bleeding that would occur after an abortion. Or maybe I just did too much damage. It seemed that I couldn't stop the bleeding, soaking through a couple of towels and several sanitary napkins. Finally, I called Carl and told him that I would need to go to the emergency room. Carl was frightened. He had no idea what would happen if an eleven year old girl showed up at the hospital bleeding from an attempted abortion. I didn't either. But the bleeding wouldn't stop and I was afraid of what would happen if we didn't.

On the way to the hospital, I told Carl that I was going to tell the medical people that I had been raped and that all of a sudden that very night I had just started bleeding. I wasn't going to say anything about the abortion or even admit that I knew I had been pregnant.

When we got to the hospital, the people in the emergency room wanted to know where my parents were. I told them that my father had been killed before I was born and that my mother was out of town where her sister was dying. I told them that Carl was my brother and that he would take care of notifying her about me being at the hospital. Perhaps because of that or that Carl was clearly an adult, or perhaps because Carl and I had taken a bunch of money out of the still mostly filled storage box to pay the hospital bill that they finally relented and began to treat me. They got the bleeding stopped, but kept me there for two more days to make certain. Of course, once I found out how much they had charged for those two days, I began to believe that they had kept me there to make a profit. Gad, it was expensive, over three thousand five hundred dollars.

Would you believe it? When I got home, my mother had not even been aware that I had not been at home. She hadn't missed me at all and didn't even ask me where I had been. She didn't know about the hospital, she knew nothing about the abortion. And I certainly wasn't going to tell her. She wasn't even home when Carl picked me up at the hospital and drove me to the house. I'm glad she wasn't, because Carl was upset all the way, crying a lot and saying it was all his fault that the baby was killed, that he should have done more, that he should quit college and take care of me. I tried to reassure him, even trying to tell him that he hadn't seduced me, it had been the other way around, but it just wasn't something he could comprehend or accept. When he dropped me off at the house and made sure I could get to the door, then he took off. He didn't even go inside with me. I thought it was that he was in a hurry to get back to college as he had already missed four days and he had to keep his GPA up if he wanted to play sports. If I had known what was going to happen, I would never have gotten out of the car.

~*~

I made it inside okay, and was elated that our mother wasn't there. Her car was gone and so was she. I made a couple of sandwiches, yes, peanut butter and jelly, but with my favorite, strawberry jelly, then I took a glass of milk and the sandwiches and went upstairs to bed. I didn't even get a chance to finish the sandwiches before I passed out.

When I woke up, sometime late in the night, the sandwiches really tasted good, although the milk was almost too warm to drink. Anyway, I needed something to wash the bread down, so I finished everything, turned over and went back to sleep. In my mind, I believed that my mother would have missed me, known that I was away for over three days, found me in bed and woke me up to find out what had happened.

That was just a pipe dream, it never happened. She didn't know I had been away and I don't think she would have cared, had she known. I was still the unwanted child.

~*~

All in all, I was reasonably content. I was able to return to school without anyone knowing what had really happened. I studied hard and my grades really shot up. At home, I was relaxed, now mostly at peace. I didn't have to fear someone coming in the door and raping me, or making me have sex with other people. Dave was gone and with our mother being gone most of the time, I could just be myself, a relaxed, at ease, at home, fairly happy, eleven year old getting closer to twelve. And then the police car drove up in our yard again.

I say in our yard. We didn't have a cement driveway, just a loose gravel drive from the main road to our front yard. The front yard was mostly gravel, so you could put a car almost anywhere that you wanted. But with the gravel it wasn't possible to drive up to our house without making noise. I heard the noise of a car and looked out. *Oh no.* I thought *What now?*

The policeman that got out of the car wasn't the same deputy that had come out before. This was a young blond-haired, tall, good-looking young policeman. He had a nice face, although he wasn't smiling as he walked up to the front door, which I had already opened.

Like the other officer he asked me where my parents were, who I was, how old I was (I lied, but only a little). I told him I was fourteen. When he found out that I was the only one home, he gave me the bad news. Carl was dead. He had committed suicide.

It was my turn. I fainted. Got the door closed just in time.

~*~

This time when I gave the news to my mother, she seemed to accept it more easily. Guess it was because she didn't care for Carl in the same way she did Dave. Or perhaps it was just because she was partly high on something when she came home. I had learned to spot someone that was high on alcohol or drugs while Dave was still alive. I don't know what she was using, it didn't have an odor and I wasn't going to get close enough to smell anything that wasn't strong.

She was less upset than I was. I don't think I really loved Carl. Now that I think about it, I don't believe that at the time I could have loved any man. To them I was just a toy and to me they were all just pigs. Nasty pigs. And in my young brain, I wasn't able to separate Carl from the rest of them.

Still, in the note he left before he shot himself, Carl left the only thing he owned to me: the old, hand-me-down car that he had been given by Dave. My mother didn't care. She had her own car and she had also sold the red car that Dave had been driving when he had the accident. Since it was almost destroyed, I don't think she got a lot out of it, but I don't think she cared much about it, just wanting to get rid of it.

Of course, now that I was twelve and slowly approaching thirteen, I knew it would be a couple or three years before I could drive. Still, I would take the keys and sit in the car. I would start up the motor and practice driving back and forth over the gravel drive and how to make u-turns in our yard. I would dream about the day when I would be able to drive myself to school or to the shops, or perhaps just off into the distance, somewhere away from this dreadful place. I remembered that I had promised Carl that I wouldn't use the little red pills so often, so it was only on special occasions that I did use one. And I did have a large supply, having grabbed every one of the oxycodone that Dave had amassed, even the stronger ones from Canada.

A couple of months after Carl had shot himself, my mother began bringing guys home with her. Most of the time it was just one man, a large man by the name of Frank. Sometimes there were others, but Frank seemed to be her favorite. I didn't like him much; I thought he looked too much like Dave. Now that I think on it, perhaps that was the reason he became my mother's favorite.

I didn't like Frank because he scared me. All the time. I would catch him staring at me, looking at my legs and my body, especially when my mother was doing something else. I tried to spend as little time alone with Frank as possible and even tried not to be there when he was with my mother. I had thought my mother was blind or somewhat dumb, but it seems that she saw more than I thought. She would talk to me, telling me that I should be nice to Frank, that he was a good man and that it was possible that he would become my father.

*Bull,* I thought. *Fathers don't look at their daughters like Frank is looking at me.* In fact, in my mind, I was aware that decent adult men never looked at twelve-year-old girls the way that Frank looked at me, so I tried to stay away as much as I can.

One day I came home from school to find Frank there alone. When I asked where my mother was, Frank said that she had gone to the grocery to buy some food for that night. He tried to move close to me, but I just turned around and ran up the stairs to my room and closed the door. (Carl had replaced the locks that Dave had removed, so I felt safe in my room)

Several hours later, I was hungry. I carefully opened my door, but didn't see anyone, so I went downstairs. When I went into the kitchen, I was surprised to see my mother. And Frank.

Without saying a word, I took the peanut butter and bread and began making a sandwich. When I reached for the strawberry jelly, Frank asked me to make a sandwich for him. When I hesitated, my mother told me that I might as well get used to obeying Frank, that he had moved in with us and they were getting married. Frank just looked at me and smirked.

*Oh no!*

~*~

My intuition was dead right. No sooner had Frank moved in than he tried to hug me any time he could. He would also pat me on my back, making sure that he touched my butt every time he did. He would paw at me, never anything overt that would upset my mother, but keeping me on the edge of panic. Rather than getting support from my mother, all she would say was, "Be nice to Frank, he is your father now." Or, "Obey Frank, he knows what's best." Or, "Do what Frank tells you. Do you want another whipping?" Or "Frank is just trying to help you. Do what he tells you."

Right! Help me? Hah.

Sure enough, it wasn't long after he moved in that I came home from school to find that only Frank was in the house. He said that my mother had some errands to run and that she would be back much later that night. I knew what was coming, there was no way out. There was no one to help, least of all a caring, loving mother. Not saying a word, I turned around and went up to my room, taking a glass of water with me. I didn't bother to lock the door, but went to my stash of little red pills and took one. Just as the oxycodone was taking effect, the door to my room opened and Frank stood there, a big grin on his face.

~*~

Okay, I'm not going to repeat all the bad things that I went through with Frank. Just remember what happened with Dave and you can imagine, except that Frank couldn't do it as often as Dave. Sometimes once a day, and sometimes maybe only three or four times a week. I didn't count, just reached for another little red pill, and closed my eyes. You might think that my mother would have gotten jealous, but there were times that she was downstairs while Frank was upstairs with me. And sometimes she was downstairs with another man while Frank was with me. Talk about a "loving" mother.

~*~

Over the next four years, there was virtually no change, except I was beginning to run low on my supply of little red pills. I learned that the pills from Canada were one hundred and sixty milligrams, almost three times as strong as the little red pills, so I was able to cut one of the larger ones into three parts. That really saved my day, increasing my hoard by two-thirds.

Another thing that happened was that I reached the age of fifteen and was able to get a learner's permit and take driver's education in school, so that by the time I was sixteen and able to get my driver's license, I knew how to drive reasonably well. And that would be the day.

Frank wanted to help me learn to drive, or at least that is what he kept saying. Actually the only times he was in my car, he was always grabbing me, poking me with his fingers, squeezing my breasts or legs. Somehow, I don't believe that helped me learn at all, but it did make me spend more time with the driving instructor from the school.

Although it seemed that it would never come, finally, it arrived.

# Part 6

Sixteen. Sixteen. Sweet, sweet sixteen. At last. What is it that the old song says, "sweet sixteen and never been kissed." Hah.

But sixteen. Able finally to drive alone, unsupervised. Able to go places and do things. For the first time in my life I was glad that I looked much older than I was. Many people had taken me for sixteen when I was only eleven. Now to look at me, one would think that I was in my early twenties, and I was only sixteen. Still, since I hadn't had a childhood, or had my childhood taken away, I had lived in hell for twelve years. And that, dear people, will age you.

Anyhow, on the day I was sixteen, I got out of bed fairly late. My mother and Frank had gone off somewhere, I don't remember where. And frankly, I didn't care, it was only important they were gone. The night before I had packed what was left of my stash and hidden it in the trunk of Carl's old car – or rather, now, my old car – and had made sure it was full of gas. Although it was an ancient car, almost as old as I am, it ran rather well. Carl had been a good mechanic and I hadn't done anything to run the car after he willed it to me.

I packed a small suitcase with most of the clothes that made me look more adult, clothes that I had bought for myself and leaving behind everything that even appeared youthful. I put those clothes bags in the trunk and then the last thing I did was to climb those trees and cut loose the bags of money. Climbing back down, skinned knees and all, I hauled the bags to the car. They filled up almost all the rear seat. But that was okay, there was not going to be any passengers going with me.

Getting in the car, I quickly turned around and then I drove down the gravel drive onto the street. I never looked back.

# Epilogue

And, so, there you have it. The story of yet another survivor of childhood sexual abuse. There is an aftermath in that at the age of sixteen, I knew that I would have to find an adult that I could rely on. I had a car full of money and a head full of dreams, but I knew that no one would listen to a teenager, no matter if she did look older. But I had a plan. I had already chosen my adult, now I just had to find him.

Charlie was the forty-first name on the list. Dave had kept records of all of the people who bought from him. I'm not sure how he got the information, but he had their names and addresses, and I had his little black book. It had been in the drawer where he kept his pills and when I took the bottles, I had grabbed the book. Didn't know what I was going to do with it at the time, but it came in handy. All I had to do was to drive to each of the addresses that Dave had amassed and wait a little while to see who lived at that address. When it wasn't the person that I was hunting, I would move on to the next address. After forty-two misses, I finally scored a bull's eye. There he was, my kindly white-haired old man, Charlie.

That was some twenty-five or so years ago. Telling you exactly when would tell you my exact age, and that is something a lady just doesn't do. And yes, I am a lady. Charlie convinced me.

Of course, it wasn't easy at first. Charlie was shocked that I was able to find out where he lived. He was even more shocked when I told him that he was going to marry me. Didn't ask, just told. I believe he was going to refuse so I mentioned that something about child abuse and minors and jail and prison and police. That got his attention. Still, he kept telling me that he was too old and I was too young and that he would act as my father and help me find a good life, and possibly a good man.

I had had all of the men I wanted. Now I wanted someone who would look after me, help me. Charlie had been kind before and I knew he was a good-hearted man. I also knew that he would be a good kind of husband, and I was right. We had fifteen years of extremely good life before Charlie died. Fifteen years of forgetting, of healing, of growing.

Before Charlie died, we managed to put most of the money that I had to work. Charlie's background had been in construction, so by wisely using the funds I had, he and I became one of the largest general contractors in the South. The first thing we built was our own home. Neither of us had ever had a home that we could actually call our own so we took particular pains to make sure we built exactly what we wanted. And the rest is history.

I said something about going through my mother's estate papers earlier. That is another reason that I can write this book now. My mother died several years ago. From Aids. Evidently, she had contracted the disease from one of her many sex partners. That must have been an awful way to die. As far as I know, there were no loved ones around when she died. Certainly not me.

Naturally, I didn't go to the funeral, I just couldn't. Nor could I forgive her. Most of the time I don't even think about her at all, just buried everything in the back of my mind. But writing these words brings it all back. She was a most pitiful person and no mother at all. But still, I wouldn't wish that on anyone, not even her.

There were a lot of people, mostly men, who felt that as a widow, especially a rich widow, that I needed a man in my life. No thanks, I had had all of the men that I could stand. And the same thing for women. They found out that I wasn't going to be a target for any of them. I guess most of them believed that Charlie was the brains and guts of our organization, but all that Charlie did was to advise a little here and there and give me the freedom to do whatever I wanted to do. Truth is, we've grown more than two hundred percent since Charlie's death. As chairman (or should it be chairwoman) of the board of a multi-million dollar operation, I believe that I have come a long way. I just wish Carl could see me now.

# After Thoughts

Most victims of childhood sexual abuse live lives that are full of stress. Virtually every professional advises the victims to obtain counseling to enable them to cope with life and to learn to face other people without shame. I don't mind admitting that I think counseling is a good thing and most helpful

On the other hand I did not get counseling. At least, I should say, professional counseling from a degreed counselor. However, I did have fifteen or so years of living a most comfortable life with the most gentle man imaginable, a time that allowed me to learn to cope with what happened, a time to learn to be a real person a person of value.

It is with that in mind that I am adding this last little bit. There are hundreds of thousands, no, even millions, of people in the United States and around the world that were victims of sexual predators when they were young. Often times by someone in the family or a close friend. Families try to hide the abuse, believing it is a stain on the family honor. In a word, bull.

For you that are or were victims, believe me when I say it's not your fault. It's not something you did, it's something that was done to you. You are not the bad person, they are. You are not worthless, they are. You are not evil, they are.

You are not guilty, they are. It's not on you, it's on them.

Remember, you are a child of God. God loves you. You are of value, you are a human being, a good human being. If you can get counseling, then great. If you can't may you be as fortunate as I have been, may you find a Charlie out there for you, and may you shine as a star for another's life.

May God bless. My prayers are with you.

PAB

Lastly, Ms. Editor, you can send any royalties that I earn to the Survivors of Childhood Sexual Abuse Foundation as you are doing with those of "My Sister and I: We Are Survivors." PAB

Keep up the faith, there is always
hope.